Mercury HeartLink
www.heartlink.com

RABBIT SUN

LOTUS MOON

RABBIT SUN

LOTUS MOON

poems by

ANDREA MILLENSON PENNER

Rabbit Sun, Lotus Moon: poems
Copyright ©2017 Andrea Millenson Penner

ISBN: 978-1-940769-63-9
Publisher: Mercury HeartLink
Silver City, New Mexico
Printed in the United States of America

Cover art and portrait photography by Meg Leonard
megleonard.com

Contact: *pennerink@gmail.com*

Poems

Preface   xv

I. THE PLEIADES

Rabbit Sun   3
Red Pen, Brown Paper   4
In My Own Ink   5
Fall Arrives Too Promptly   6
Ode to Sweaters   7
Home for a High School Reunion   8
Strawberry Oblivion   10
Who Needs to Learn Whose Language?   12
West Coast Summer Moonrise   13
Milk   14
Queen of the Car Club   15
Two in Their Own Time   16

II. CASSIOPEIA

Her Chimayo Jacket   21
San Francisco 3:00 a.m.   22
The World Is Not Your Size   23
Sandia Mountain Lullaby   24
Upside-Down World   25
Desert Solitude   26
Trickster Corn, or How the Clouds First Came to Be   27
Lunch at the Seafood Paradise   28

You Were Not Thinking of Her   30

Longing   32

Bury Me Under the Chocolate Flower   33

Dostoyevsky and Pajamas   34

III. URSA MAJOR

Virga   39

Earth Meditation   40

Morning After First Rain   41

Happy Merry Christmas   42

Morning Coffee on the Deck   45

Blue Day, Black Crow   46

The Prophets Call Three-One-One   48

Headed North   50

Lee's Tea House   51

Versailles in a Teacup   54

A Footbridge Spans the River of Lost Souls   55

Six Short Dialogues   56

IV. CYGNUS

On the Edge of the Lagoon   61

Bastille Day   62

Winter Sky Stories   63

The Great Ultimate   64

Mary Ponders the Word Made Flesh   65

Luminarias   66

A Poet's Cairn   68

Ordinary Bliss   70
She Did Not Expect   72
Igneous Love   73
Riding a Lazy Horse in Costa Rica   74
Division of Labor   76

V. ORION

Silly Poem Composed in Traffic   81
Holding You   82
Landlords   83
Love Note   84
Out to Sea   86
The One That Got Away   87
Under Another Sky   88
Perspective   89
Eve, in the *Bosque*   90
Taste the Morning   91
Aging in Tree Pose   93
Lotus Moon   94

Acknowledgments   96
About the Author   99

With Gratitude

to New Mexico's poets and artists, writers
and teachers whose labors inspire us
to be our best selves for good causes;
to my family and friends, an ever-widening circle;
y a mi media naranja.

PREFACE

Dear Reader:

If you were sitting near my kitchen window, in view of the Sandia Mountains, I would pour you a steaming cup of tea, coffee, or cocoa, and share this book with you. Your attention might be diverted by a clutch of quail skittering across the gravel or by daylight's sudden shift from ordinary to golden in New Mexico's late afternoon. Several poems depict such moments when the natural world offers itself unreservedly as setting and sustenance. Others recall events and experiences, relationships and landscapes that have marked my journey and awakened me to what is important in this one precarious and precious life between earth and sky.

Several months ago, I emailed a draft manuscript to my sister, Laura, who lives in Australia. She responded by text message: "I am always looking for little clues in each poem to help me understand your perspective and perceptions." Laura and I have not lived in the same country since she left California at age twenty (when I was twelve) to follow her heart to New Zealand. Long before the days of personal computers and cell phones, we corresponded by aerogram—a thin blue sheet of paper that, when folded and sealed, transformed into a pre-paid envelope for cheap, overseas correspondence. Weighty emotions were tucked invisibly between the lines.

Divergent and intertwined, our double-helix relationship has twisted through half a century—separated by oceans, united by love. In the early years, postal strikes Down Under caused agonizing delays. I would rush home from school to check the mailbox, immediately calling mom at work to report an air-mail delivery. At fifteen, on saved babysitting and birthday money, I traveled alone to Australia for a summer (their winter). Two years later, Laura and her husband arrived just in time for my high school graduation.

Gaps between visits lengthened. We raised children (and Laura grieved the sudden loss of her nine-year-old daughter); we went to church (or graduate school); we stayed happily married (or struggled to do so); each moved several times. We updated our address books and wrote many letters. Sometimes we enclosed photographs or exchanged cassette tapes of our young ones' voices singing songs and telling stories in foreign accents. Only occasionally did we speak by phone.

Tomorrow always reaches my sister's continent first. There are no pueblo villages in Queensland, no rain forests in New Mexico. She walks daily on the beach; I hike in the desert foothills. Connected by a common ancestry and history—making the same bran muffin and chicken soup recipes, cracking eggs the kosher way, and cutting the ends off vegetables—we presume a measure of familiarity even as our lives evolve separately. Our family tree is not oak, but aspen, a rhizome traveling far and deep, reproducing itself in distant, sunny places.

No wonder Laura and I still find each other mysterious. Whether by email, text, or phone, we continue to delight, surprise, and baffle one another. We are neither sisters who fight nor sisters who finish each other's sentences. Instead, we ask questions, listen for answers, and look for clues. If neighbors, we would be walking buddies. She would delight in pink clouds above the headland and I would know she was thinking of her daughter. Or I would stop, finger to lips, to indicate doe and fawn behind a juniper tree; she would perceive my latest maternal worry.

These poems, each one an aerogram, dispatch enfolded blue thoughts (to you and my sister) that may arrive months or years after the incident, idea, or feeling they disclose. Open them carefully to glimpse the landscapes that move me, the territory of my heart. May you also discover new continents and recognize familiar constellations. The stars remain, even when we can't see them.

With love,

Andi

I. THE PLEIADES

Rabbit Sun

Sun stays one step ahead of winter
hopping above mammatus clouds,
just out of reach.

Rabbit makes morning rounds
        greets the day
        pops from rock to chamisa to cactus
twitches with anticipation
twists ears this way and that
        stops in deer tracks and sniffs.

Single snowflakes flit
one here   one there
white-winged ice fairies
ephemeral as fireflies in summer

Snow crystals
melt before touching shadows.
Rabbit darts under Apache Plume.

We hold each other
praying the sun will stay
        one step ahead of winter.

RED PEN, BROWN PAPER

A writer without her notebook
is a coffee drinker
with a mug of green tea
        a rummaged red pen
        and a recycled brown napkin
next to the tire shop
waiting in the winter sun
to erase the evidence
of that day   when she jumped the curb
in a slow hurry.
How easy it would be
to ignore the gash—
tires don't bleed, after all—
and to deny that the sun's rays
        so warm on her neck
do not irradiate skin
and that no one she knows
is close to dying. Only love
in the world today, please,
scratched in red ink.
Only patience in the clerks' voices
while she waits
for two new tires
to keep her safe and balanced
at seventy-five on the highway
when the sun is in her eyes.

IN MY OWN INK

At a beach café
on the sandy curve
of a Basque bay
we enjoy
a steaming platter
of *chipirones en su tinta,*
a local delicacy.
Squid in its own ink
lies in blue-black liquid
on a bed of white rice.

I, too, am prepared
and served
in my own ink—
clouded
by memory,
inscribed
by the past.
I write,
floating
on white sheets.

Fall Arrives Too Promptly

Unfashionably early
autumn knocks
at precisely four o'clock—
bitter November cold
bursts the door
scatters students
professors and papers
in a dozen dark directions.
The empty campus
provides scant cover
from the slanted rain.
Whistling wind
resurrects
pungent scents of
long forgotten autumns
        naked trees and—

Brrrrr!
too cold
to entertain
thoughts
of

        you.

ODE TO SWEATERS

To cashmere and cable knit
to rough scratchy Scottish wool
and trendy recycled cotton blends
to sweaters that fit and baggy favorites
to jackets, coats, hats, and scarves—
glorious silk scarves—Oh! but I digress.
To turtleneck sweaters and mock turtlenecks,
V-necks, and cowl necks. To cardigans,
belted sweaters, and cozy sweaters—
dress sweaters and sweater dresses!
To hand-knit jumpers and crocheted vests.
To sweaters with pockets and sweaters with sleeves
long enough to roll over one's chilled hands.
To sweaters for cuddling—
soft soft sweaters to burrow in and
sweaters to take off when the fire is warm.
Handed-down and handed-up sweaters
moth-eaten   patched   and darned
sweaters that lose their shape when you wash them
and sweaters that shrink when you dry them.
House sweaters you wear because your mother is cold
sweaters you borrowed and kept
sweaters you loaned and lost.
Sweaters
that smell of home.

Home for a High School Reunion

I walk my old neighborhood again today.
What compels me to re-chart these streets, forty years later?
Perhaps I have missed the fused scent of citrus and jasmine.

The "Jesus Saves" house still sags in its sandy front yard
where faded surfboards—fins buried, tips pointing toward
Orange County heaven—proclaim Rest-in-Peace messages.

Friendly roses grace the church walkway,
climb the cinder-block wall behind which once hid
the preacher's daughter and me, and her cigarettes.

Different boys bicycle through the same alleys—
fat one pedals, skinny one rides the handlebars—
propelled by adolescent energy.

Familiar street names mark unrecognizable intersections;
only a block from my old junior high school,
where a new Vietnamese café serves *beignets*.

No more dusty bargins on a Main Street.
Gentrified pedestrian mall and farmers' market—
Orange-blossom honey, beet greens, ripe avacoados, and
crocheted hats.

Oh, what we would have given as teen girls
to have flirted with these fine Guatemalan farm boys
and their young fathers, and ridden home, baskets brimming.

Disintegrating Styrofoam cups float in avenue gutters.
Taco wrappers and a used condom decorate a bus-stop.
A curly purple ribbon, one end tied to a dead balloon,

strangles a healthy weed in a sidewalk crack.
I keep walking past familiar school yards, and chain-link fences,
steel arms that protected and thwarted me.

Present illuminates past
reminds me why I left
        why I keep returning.

STRAWBERRY OBLIVION

Faceless brown farm workers
appeared in season
drifting with coastal fog
into hidden suburbs, apartment
warrens behind shopping malls,
or trailers at the far edge of strawberry fields
away from the wide California boulevards
that whisked us past their muddy toil.
In straw hats or sweaty bandannas
they transformed vast vacant lots into
tilled, plastic-protected fertile earth.
Backs bent, they tended the young plants
coaxed the fruit to maturity.

Each May
the word S T R A W B E R R I E S
materialized, red letters
on whitewashed shacks
Open/Abierto alongside a sea of green.
Our parents drove slowly up dirt driveways
pointed, nodded, and exchanged carefully counted cash
struck a deal for fresh pints and flats.
We sat in the back holding the wooden crates
on our laps. Greedy for tart sweetness
hungry for dessert (whipped cream!)
we gave no thought to those families
who worked the fields together.
What did we know of migrant labor?
Fingers unstained
we did not speak the language
of Dolores Huerta or Cesar Chavez.

We had no solidarity with those
who picked our lettuce, our grapes
whose children inhaled pesticides
and missed school.
We had no cause or fight
but our own.

WHO NEEDS TO LEARN WHOSE LANGUAGE?

We need to help students and parents cherish and preserve the ethnic and cultural diversity that nourishes and strengthens this community—and this nation.
                                                    —Cesar Chavez

He fidgets in his seat
impatient for the teacher, *la maestra,*
to call on him.
He stutters and stammers
in English and Spanish.
La maestra waits
as he rummages.
Holding a toy car in each hand,
he narrates yesterday's accident, imitates the siren,
does not cry.
He expects his teacher's sympathy
but she claps her hands, delighted by his storytelling attempt,
and nods to the next child in the circle.

On the playground, far from *los maestros,*
sus compañeros console him.
A little girl reaches out her hand. *Pobrecito.*
Lo siento, says his buddy.

Why won't those kids assimilate?
asks his teacher.
Look how they stick together,
declares another.

WEST COAST SUMMER MOONRISE

Couples stroll the pier,
arms linked. They turn
to search for first-starlight
in their partners'

eyes. Tired fishermen
carry empty buckets
to the parking lot,
poles balanced

on slack shoulders.
California teens slide hands
into each other's back pockets
isolated by pounding

surf. Lunatic preacher
wears heavy chain
rebukes crowd of bemused
skeptics for their bondage

to sin. Children laugh, joke,
lick sweet drips
of creamy innocence
on the curved coastline.

Madcap moon rises above it all,
and smiles at its own reflection.

MILK

Syllable count based on the Fibonacci sequence

"There
are
crumbs in
the carton!"
my sister accused.
"Did you pour back your milk after
dipping your Oreos and drinking out of the glass?"
"Of course not. Why would I do that?"
I lied to my sis.
"He did it."
Just a
small
fib.

Queen of the Car Club

Old cars ascend the hill in single file.
In each at least one mourner, maybe two—
All are dressed in black, a few in style
Adorned with pink for Sylvia, her hue.
The vintage Chevys and Buicks pay homage due
To her for whom the men had prayed with tears
As cancer took her smiles, her life, her years.

As cancer took her life, her years too few
Her friends had stood beside her night and day
Always at least one daughter, maybe two—
Exchanging laughter even while they prayed.
Through tears they proffered smiles and pink bouquets.
Sylvia named her favorite classic cars
'Tween morphine dreams of driving past the stars.

On morphine dreams she sailed away too soon
Though cancer kept her fighting to the end.
We climb the grassy green in ones and twos
To honor mother, sister, daughter, friend.
We miss her high-beam smile, so we pretend
To hear her laughing at the shining chrome
Of the classy ride that finally takes her home.

Two in Their Own Time

I. Coastal California
We anticipated your arrival as best we could
timing the conception
to fit our plans
by trying, repeatedly
to produce the desired result at a reasonable time.
Such hubris to think
we could direct November's wind
from February's shadow.
Twins were possible
but you emerged alone
round and full
in your own time
after hours of labor that began at home
and ended with the help of a night nurse who exclaimed
"Let's get this baby out!"
Six days past due
long fingers and toes
head full of sable hair emanating from two whorls
a strong, sturdy self
gazing out from grey-green eyes
conceived of slate clouds and winter surf
wrapped in meaning
before we named you—
peace and worthy of love—
you embodied solace
grasped life.

II. Northern Arizona
Your heels pushed against my ribs.
Sometimes a pressed foot or fist stretched my belly.
Our friends bet on your length, weight, arrival date,
and on my ultimate circumference.

You were so active and insistent
I was certain you'd come early;
you nestled, deeper, snuggling
and burrowing securely
shielded from summer heatwave, days passing slowly
two, then five, then the doctor's order to induce
by day seven if you did not volunteer.

One week late
artificially prompted
you twisted into the world with eyes already open—
        the nurse gasped when you looked at her!—
your torso twice wrapped
by a thirty-two inch long umbilical cord.
You nuzzled into my neck
and curled up in my arms.
Named for ancestors,
your life began
in safety, health, and comfort
before you were thrust into a world
that would only later quake and flood
and break apart.

II. Cassiopeia

HER CHIMAYO JACKET

for Martha

Thou shalt not covet thy mother-in-law's vintage jacket.
Oh, but I do: tailored Chimayo Blanket on cedar in guest closet.

Red wool sleeves says, "touch me."
Sterling silver buttons boast, "we're older than you."

She lets me try it on, smoothing the yoke and back.
Heavy wool wonders if I can bear its weight.

Two square front pockets hide promises and candy wrappers.
One red collar turns up its tongue, murmuring secrets.

"My uncle bought this for me," she says. "I felt so proud in it!
Father would not let me wear it to church."

Now her jacket comes home to New Mexico with me
retracing the lines of its design.

* * *

Years later, on dementia's doorstep,
she recalls the jacket but loses the thread.

The 1940s. She travels with her parents—
Route 66 from Kansas to California via New Mexico.

In the dusty trading post, the woven jacket
draws her deeper into its warp and weft.

San Francisco 3:00 A.M.

Twenty-first floor
hotel room window
frames Coit Tower
emasculated by fog
diminutive church spires float
on a sea of blinking pink neon
and soft yellow halos.
City luminescence
sleepless poets and priests
pray for peace
pay for sin.

THE WORLD IS NOT YOUR SIZE

Try as you might
to make it fit
the world is not
your size.

Stand on your tip-toes
to peer through a telescope
at Andromeda, the Milky Way,
or our neighborly moon.

Hold out your arms
S-T-R-E-T-C-H your wingspan
imagine yourself an albatross
gliding over a great ocean.

Examine tiny organisms
through a microscope.
Marvel as the hairy little critters
bump into one another.

Scale the mountain in search of grandeur
or insignificance.

Squat on your heels to study the mysterious wildflowers
thriving at twelve thousand feet
on the Colorado plateau.
These illuminated bottle-brush blossoms
resemble a distant galaxy—
each crimson spine tipped with iridescent yellow,
one hundred worlds balanced in neat rows.
How did they come to flourish in this unlikely place?

How is it that you are here
        at all?

SANDIA MOUNTAIN LULLABY

Three Sandia* granite boulders align
in our back yard
perfectly placed   between juniper   and scrub oak.
Guests often hesitate
then ask, "Did you *put* those there?"

Slumbering old watermelon woman
from whom these mountain bones tumbled
looms over us in summer
ignores us in winter.
Patient with human audacity,
she may bide her time
for another thirty million years
until she decides
to shed her sides
in the next great upheaval,
to fling her plutonic quartz, feldspar, and mica
ribs down upon our long forgotten remains.

Or perhaps tomorrow
she will shake herself awake
pull further from her former lover
the Rio Grande   widen their rift
and down will come mountain
        house guests
           and all.

Sandia is the Spanish word for "watermelon." The mountains, it
is said, were named either for their momentary watermelon-red
appearance at sunset, or for the green-striped gourds that grow
on its alluvial fans.

Upside-Down World

We startle awake
at the news.
Life turns upside-down.
Antique cups and saucers
plummet from shelves
splintering into pink and white shards
as sharp as sucked candy canes.
Flowers freefall from Waterford vases
petals and pollen, leaves and stems
mingle with stale cake crumbs and poppy seeds
shaken from the cracks in the floorboards.
A handblown decanter of crème de menthe
pours a sticky green river
no one could skate away on
while black vinyl records
slip their dust jackets,
roll across the ceiling, shatter into licorice spikes.
Glass explodes.

Where is Mrs. Pigglewiggle when you need her?
With her magic hump and topsy-turvy house,
ceiling fans for lazy Susans
and an attic in the basement,
our storybook wise woman
always had the remedy for trouble.

But we are on our own
this time
setting right the wrongs
setting wrongs in stone.

Desert Solitude

Rock layers
expose basin shale

labyrinthine sand
blows through earth's dendritic veins

desiccated bone
crumbles underfoot—

future
dust.

Fossils
know.

Inhale
fear.
Swallow
anxiety.

Consume *what-ifs*
before you, too, vanish.

Grind smooth your gastrolith—
visceral worry stone
polished
by years of patient practice.

TRICKSTER CORN, OR HOW THE CLOUDS FIRST CAME TO BE

Syllable count based on the Fibonacci sequence

Blue
corn
grew tall.
Coyote
snuck into the field
stealthily picked silk-covered ears
stole away. Chased by Crow and on the run, Coyote
leaped skyward—vaulted into elliptical orbit, followed gravity, hoping to
land safely with purloined treasure. But he lost his grip
and dropped all stalks into the Sun—
consumed by fire—
pop, pop, pop!
Sky filled
with
clouds.

LUNCH AT THE SEAFOOD PARADISE

Crushed velvet slipcovers conceal worn chairs
in their favorite Chinese restaurant
on a forgotten corner in California
several miles from her father's home.
Plates and cutlery clatter in busboys' dishpans
while the dim sum matrons
peddle expensive delicacies in tones
as shrill as their carts' squeaking wheels.
"You want scallop dumpling?"
"How you like duck feet?"

Hostesses shout names to seat
the lunch crowd. Acrylic chandeliers brighten
the chaos. Large family parties talk over each other.
Young boys play drums with chopsticks.
"WAS IT SO NOISY IN BEIJING?" She repeats,
leaning toward him over the pale pink tablecloth.
"Not this bad," he says, adjusting his hearing aid.

They study their menus. He tells the waiter
"Shrimp with Lobster Sauce"
one of his two favorites.
She orders something spicy.

This time tea and rice are served steaming hot
as if someone remembered
their displeasure months ago
on their last visit.

Decades ago, her engineer father had ventured to China,
marveled at the Terra Cotta Army of Xi'an
and the beautiful Forbidden City. He dubbed
Beijing the "City of Amazing Grays."

In Shanghai, he and the delegation watched as uniformed waiters
woke up and crawled from under the tables
to serve breakfast.

At the Seafood Paradise
ghosts sleep at their feet.
She slurps sweet and sour soup.
He enjoys the last shrimp.
Sometimes the spirits dine with them
or wait near the door.
She sees them reflected in his glasses
when he looks up at her.

Together they break their fortune cookies.
"Maybe next time,"
he says,
"We should try the dim sum."

YOU WERE NOT THINKING OF HER

You were not thinking of her
gone these eight years
when the small bird-shaped rock
attracted you. The artifact resembled
     a pet bird
one that fits in the hollow of your hand
or sits on a tiny swing
seen through a cage—
the kind of bird you would stroke
gently with only the lightest
touch of your index finger
her fierce eyes peering back at you
the same way your mother stared, unblinking
imprisoned in her rigid but living body.

Cradle the bird-rock
in your palm.
Recognize an artisan's intent
beneath impacted clay.
The bird's delicate head
forms the decorated handle
of a tiny carved lamp.
You imagine its circular depressions
filled with olive oil
caressing a cotton wick—
flame, an offering.
You rubbed oil into your mother's skin
and uttered wick-smoke prayers
to release her.
Perched on bed pillows,
she wailed from her throat.
Inner light waned.

Feel her weight in your palm,
trace simple, rough engravings.
Close your eyes.
Enter a clamorous tent, a prayer room,
a cage.

You were not thinking of her.

LONGING

I helped you dress
for the recital
in ecru tights, soft gray leotard,
and delicate rose tutu.
You tied the ribbons
on your pale pink ballet slippers
using bunny ears—one, two, crisscross, pull—
just the way I taught you.
I brushed your long brown hair,
twisted thick curls into a *chignon.*
You were becoming the dancer
I had longed to be.

> Enacting ballet school daydreams—
> *grand jetés* in the living room
> *pirouettes* down the hall—
> while my sister practiced piano,
> I was told, "No, darling,
> you're too frail."

This picture frame
is dusty
but I see you clearly
in leotard, tights, and tutu
preparing for your final dance
sweet lips
long lashes
eyes focused
on tying the bow
just so.

BURY ME UNDER THE CHOCOLATE FLOWER

for the fragrant *Berlandiera lyrata*

Bury me under the chocolate flower
scatter me to the sea
lower me into loamy earth
covered with aspen leaves

sift me with the sand of a southern shore
float me on a twig in the creek
hold me up to the arctic wind
blowing down from the highest peak

and I'll find my way to the midnight sky
to silence between the stars
with my arms encircling the galaxies
the universe expanding my heart

so bury me under the chocolate flower
scatter me to the sea
release me in a river's meander

let me choose my eternity.

DOSTOYEVSKY AND PAJAMAS

*For the mystery of human existence lies not in just
staying alive, but in finding something to live for.*
—from *The Brothers Karamazov*

He wonders:
How did I lose my balance?
When did time pass without my knowing?
Why did I let this happen?

He used to walk unaided, on toes and heels.
When did he succumb to wheels?
How did his ears grow plastic inserts
with tiny filaments and switches?
Why did he exchange Dostoyevsky for *Jeopardy*?

When did his vision deteriorate and membranes dry—
scheduled tears dropped in
or eyes watering at random?
How did his bladder become a drainage bag?
Why has his voice declined?
When did his caregiver become his conscience
reminding him to drink more water, take a nap, and shave?

Each night, he loosens time from his wrist
removes his second set of eyes
places his ears in their container
and his spare teeth
in their cup. He slides off his slippers,
releases his stable grip.

Other hands take over.

They put him in his pajamas,
adjust his pillows,
and tuck him into bed.
After the nightly tears are dropped in,
he closes his eyes,
freed from his own Grand Inquisition
of hows and whens and whys.
He alternately sleeps and wakes
and dreams of another tomorrow.

III. Ursa Major

VIRGA

We wait
tantalized.

Charged air rumbles
in the steel-blue distance.

The heady scent of moisture
entices us outdoors.

Promising gray clouds
extend tendrils toward earth.

The desert is greedy
face upturned for rain.

It may not come.

We know
it will not last.

Note: Every summer, the desert Southwest teases us with
virga, the formation of clouds whose visible streaking rain
evaporates before reaching the ground.

EARTH MEDITATION

The earth is turning
The earth is turning on her elliptical path
The earth is turning on her elliptical path around the sun
    tipping her hat to the moon and bowing to the stars

The earth is spinning
The earth is spinning silently through black space
The earth is spinning silently through black space and
luminous time
    speeding imperceptibly

Now the earth is groaning
The earth is groaning with sorrow
The earth is groaning with the sorrows of all her children
    riding on her back
    riding on her back through black holes, warped time
    speeding imperceptibly toward they know not what

The earth is turning
The earth is turning into a ball
The earth is turning into a ball of ice and fire
The earth is turning into a ball of bitter heat and burning cold
    collapsing toward the center

The earth is spinning
The earth is spinning her web
The earth is spinning her web of seasons, eras, and epochs
    spinning through luminous time and dark space
    spinning the filament of sorrows
    weaving the fiber of gauzy grace

MORNING AFTER FIRST RAIN

Pre-dawn heat vibrates
above the *sipapu*,
their annual emergence place.

Sunlight strikes the opening.

Up from the lower world
Flying Ants by thousands
surge from their humid hole
in cracked concrete.
Shimmering and radiant,
they crawl through gravel
or flash up and away
on crystalline wings.
Curve-billed Thrasher and Whiptail Lizard
discover the sudden bounty.
Lizard stakes his claim
on the fissure
with perfect flicks of his tongue.
Thrasher hops, runs, darts among rocks
pecking single Ants one after another.
Spying her Lizard competition,
Thrasher ascends to a brittle branch
swoops   beak open
swallows her share, midflight.
The fittest Ants escape the feast.

HAPPY MERRY CHRISTMAS

One hundred-forty-four miles from home
to the Pueblo. Sun warms the car,
each highway mile a new landscape
and an old memory.

Listen to an interview with the Governor
on Southern Ute Tribal radio until out of range.
Native DJs on KUNM's "Singing Wire" play shout-outs
and banter about whose mom's fry bread is the best.

Hum along with "O Holy Night" sung in Navajo
and tap the steering wheel
to a pow wow drum song
with a "Happy Merry Christmas" refrain.

Pull off the red canyon road.
Squeeze into a narrow dirt parking space
between two large pickups
on the east side of the plaza.

Should leave coat in the car
but can't quite believe
in winter sun
even on this immaculate day.

Follow drumbeats and singing
to a small crowd, southwest of the Middle.
Stand in the warmth, inhaling dust and juniper smoke.
Scan the crowd for my host.

A wrinkled man greets me,
tells me that over there, inside, are tables
full of every good thing to eat—"*posole*, chile, bread, sweets—
everything. You go eat," he says, pointing his lips toward the
house.

Stand outside—happily the only white woman in line.
Inside, the wood stove radiates comforting heat.
Colorful striped blankets, ribbons, silk and cotton scarves,
Christmas ornaments, and tinsel decorate the walls and ceiling.

Swaddled Infant figure rests on a table among candles, corn pollen,
silver crosses, wood carvings, folded bills, and loose change.
        Quietly pay Him my respects
then ask after my friend, but no one knows him.

In the next room, benches line both sides of a long table,
every inch covered with platters, bowls, and casseroles—
steaming stew, teriyaki chicken, yams, oven bread, red and green chile.
Aproned grandmothers shuttle dishes, pour fruit punch and coffee.

A mother and daughter sit on either side of me.
Offer to move so they can sit together—
"No," says the mother, "she sees me all the time."
They both giggle and dish out more pink marshmallow salad.

Leave the table shortly after the drummer
and singers file quietly out the back door.
Walk to the plaza, past children chasing puppies.
Many chairs set up, but few onlookers have returned.

Stand near a mustard yellow house on the northwest side of the Middle.
Drumming begins in the east.
A chorus of men's voices rumbles, rises, and falls
behind a higher summoning call. People gather.

Two buffalo escort a third impressive creature
adorned with thick headdress of turkey feathers.
"She is the Mother of All Game," a man next to me murmurs
before he and his long white hair withdraw.

At least two dozen deer and ram dancers join her
bent on wooden front legs, Sun shields on their backs,
bodies rich with bells, sashes, antlers, horns,
feathers, and silver bracelets set with polished turquoise.

Six eagles, wings outstretched and dipping, lead a herd
of yellow antelope with small horns, short tails, and creamy hides.
A second chorus of men with drums follow a
Chief figure in full headdress. He carries a large hunting bow.

Pueblo housetops display white-wire Christmas trees, Santas,
and reindeer decorated with lights and shiny garland.
Children's voices sound like the aroma of sweet kettle corn.
New arrivals fill every chair to overflowing with babies and blankets.

Dozens of women step forward simultaneously
gently shaking cornmeal-filled fists, hands close, chest high
until a crescendo of bells precede silence.
In unison, the women withdraw into the crowd.

Drumming resumes. The herd moves up the Middle, east to west.
A tall, big-bellied man in denim jacket and sunglasses turns around
to ask "Where you from?"
Drove down from Farmington, but not really from *there.*
"You coming back tomorrow? They'll be dancing again."
No, only today.

"Then stand in front, little one," he chuckles, "so you can see better.
You seen the Infant, yet? That was my family. Every year, the Infant
stays with a different household. They host the feast.
Maybe the Infant will go stay with you," he winks,
"and next Christmas we'll all show up in Farmin'ton."
We share a good laugh.

Still smiling, walk to my car.
Drive the hundred-forty-four miles home.
Every mile a drum beat.
Every mesa a song.
Every cloud a prayer.
Happy Merry Christmas.

Morning Coffee on the Deck

Winter sun creates
long shadows in slanted rows.

Quail calls punctuate
a thrasher's sweet ten-note song
that rises and repeats above the whirr
of furnace and thrum of morning traffic.
Distant jet rumbles
       across a lingering moon.
Small gray juniper titmouse chatters
from nearby tree
       look-at-me   look-at-me   look-at-me
Coiffed in stylish tuft—
backlit in a silver dandelion hat gone to seed—
light face, dark eyes, and pointy beak tip toward me.

Coffee cup empty,
I go inside, get ready for work.
Today I will try
to rise above the noise
and pay attention
       pay attention
            pay attention.

BLUE DAY, BLACK CROW

The paved road from Eldorado to Madrid via Galisteo
narrows as it turns right at old Galisteo Church
and snakes through a dry arroyo past a Watch for Water sign
where you could stand in New Mexico's bright blue heat
all day—and never see a drop.
Dwellers in parched landscapes watch for many things—
signs of rain, lizard tracks,
the faintest hint of friendship.

At Cemetery Hill
the road divides Catholics from Protestants,
but low stone walls and locked wooden gates
cannot protect the graves.
Blowing sand and harsh sun
fade markers and whither blue plastic flowers.
Only illusion separates
the living from the dead.

Striped pavement slithers west across
arid grassy basins
curves north and south, sometimes
eyeing the snow-covered peaks above Santa Fe
sometimes biting the indigo heels of the Cerrillos Hills,
eyeing the eastern slopes of the Sandias.
Undulant asphalt conforms to harsh beauty
born of earth's internal gnashing.

In Madrid, you wander into a small soap-scented shop.
"It's a blue day," you tell the owner-artist
as you pay for purchases:
        a simple silver band set with lapis lazuli—
                clouds swirling inside a small blue universe—
        a sprig of lavender
        and an unframed mystical blue painting—
                a backward glancing blue-black crow
                who knows more than he's telling
                about where the road goes
                from here.

The Prophets Call Three-One-One

I.   Cloudburst at the corner of Pennsylvania and Central—
Small man in baggy suit
mutters pronouncements at passing cars
that splash gutter water as he pushes his shopping cart
up the sidewalk facing traffic.
The wobbly wheels struggle under voluptuous
trash bags, the sum of his possessions.

II.   Elijah summers at the university duck pond,
winters in its library. He always smiles, looks out
for me between classes. The ducks and I share bread with
the prophet. We talk about books and trade family stories.
I introduce him to my classmate on an autumn afternoon.
Months later, they chat amiably near the reference desk
on a cold, rainy night while I pack my books at closing time.
Together we leave the library in obscurity.
                                        Where do the prophets sleep?

III.   Late one cold night, drug store parking lot,
woman approaches from the shadows,
asks for money. I hurry past in coat over pajamas
to buy cough syrup for my kids
with no spare money of my own—only enough cash
for the smallest generic-brand bottle
until payday—I tell her I am sorry.
"You'll be sorry as shit!" she predicts.

IV.   Duke City responds with bright blue signs:
Call 311 If You Need HELP with Food or Shelter.
This town does not discriminate. We invite all homeless veterans
and recovering addicts, all freed felons who did their time, all

teens who traded domestic violence for street corners— call
from this spot using the cell phone you can't afford. Call
from the home phone your parents won't let you use. Call
from the office phone at the job you can't get. Call 311.
Don't stand on this median preaching tolerance.
Don't hold signs at city intersections. Don't
remind us that we have failed you.

> *Who will answer the prophet's call?*

HEADED NORTH

Driving home tonight
  after nightfall, in the rain
  north on Tramway
  paralleling the city's backbone
Listening to Prudencio's music—
  the CD he autographed for my 55th birthday—
     I'm a worried wonder
     I worry 'round in circles
His lyrics lull me into a state of grace—
  that place where life fractures
  a cracked fibula, a broken window
  and it's still okay.
Lightning chooses that
  moment
  to flash inside the clouds
  behind Rincon Ridge
Jagged silhouette
  against a yellow sky
  for a split second
Reminds me that you are home
  waiting for me
  and I am headed
  in the right direction.

LEE'S TEA HOUSE

Somewhere in North Florida cracker country
down the road from Jesus
she owns the shack of her dreams—
a someday tea house, a comfort station.
On her family's best mismatched china
she'll serve cups of sympathy with marmalade biscuits
because *that's what people really want*, she tells me,
someone to listen.

We sit at a large, round table in a hotel lobby
while she rummages through her denim bag
pulling out pens, sticky notes,
a bound copy of the U.S. Constitution—
          I got to get myself organized.
Her wallet falls open, spilling
business cards and folded
scraps of paper, a plastic sleeve with photographs:
          Here it is—she produces a faded image
shovel and rake lean against
small decaying building
other farm implements lie scattered,
planted beneath the trees.
          Someday I'll reclaim my land.

                    *   *   *

She holds my hand.
          They don't know what happened to me.
          I was three months in the dungeon they
          call a nursing pavilion. I'm a healthy woman—
          at least I was. I've walked the John Muir Trail.
          Now I can't drive. I doubt I'll ever
          build my tea house.
          Can you believe they took my car?
          If they can do that to my car

what can they do to me?
That's why I'm reading up on my rights.
After I'm gone, they can take my daddy's house.

She keeps a yellowed newspaper clipping
with captioned picture of a dignified two-story house:
"Mr. Henry Jackson builds his grand home for $15,000
at the corner of 3rd Street and 6th Avenue."
It's not the Biltmore, but it's home.

       *   *   *

Did I tell you I take the phone off the hook
for the New York Review of Books,
close the blinds, and curl up in my Queen Anne
for the whole day   sipping tea and reading?
Apparently, that's where I was when my busy-body
neighbor found me   but I don't remember.

Lee announces that she traveled to India
     before the Beatles made it popular
and frequented Berkeley's bookstores and coffee shops
as a happy faculty wife.
     I don't know if you know this about men, dear....
she confides, recounting his infidelities
and her escape on a solo cross-country drive.
At my mention of New Mexico she says
     Oh what a wonderful place—
     and of course we all love O'Keeffe.

Her regrets? She never drove the blue highways
through Arizona's painted desert, heard the wolves howl
when she camped in the wild Minnesota woods, or witnessed
a New England autumn.
     Other than that, I've done just about everything
     a woman needs to do in this life.

*   *   *

Lee smoothes her unruly white hair
adjusts her glasses and scoops strewn
belongings into her denim bag—
    I got to get organized.
She grabs her cane, gives me a kiss,
and strides toward the nearest exit.

VERSAILLES IN A TEACUP

Unbidden but not unwelcome
he returns from far-away France
bearing neither jewels nor promises
but gilded blue glass,
        Versailles in a teacup
        the Seine in a saucer
fragile as her dreams
of lush mazes
hedges disguise the path
winding deeper into the greens
and violets over the Giverny bridge
where Monet's lilies still grow
and float unperturbed.

The French cup joins
glass and china trophies.
Not enough to own—
one must also display,
be admired.

She serves her mother weak tea
in an old lover's cup—
drink this!
Her daughters scald
their tongues on steeped Darjeeling
not daring to complain while
questioning their mother's choices.

Hands too unsteady to hold
a single cup or command the distance
from saucer   to lips
her life poured generously
steaming and sweet and fragrant
now cold
leaves a brown rim
a swirled stain.

A Footbridge Spans the River of Lost Souls

steel scalene triangles
lean recklessly
a framework
forged at fragile angles

from distant origins
their perpendicular lives
intersected in this unlikely plane
precarious passage
between then and now
there and here

then yesterday
from opposite sides
they passed each other
without saying hello
or waving goodbye
        bonds broke

friends fell away

Six Short Dialogues

Inspired by a six-panel egg tempera painting by Eliza Schmid

I. Snake and Rodent
>Snake: Slow down, brother.
>Rodent: You startled me.
>Snake: Stay awhile.
>Rodent: . Look, a roadrunner!

II. Male and Female
>She: Do you want to talk about it? *(silence)*
>He: We already talked.

III. Man, Woman, and Child
>Man: We want what's best for you.
>Woman: We want you to be happy.
>Child: Leave me alone.

IV. Fox and Snake
>Fox (philosophically): Cada cabeza es un mundo.
>Snake (hungrily):   Y el mundo es mio.
>*Zorro (filosoficamente)*: Each head is a world.
>*Culebra (con hambre)*: And the world is mine.

V. Poet and Artist
>Said the poet to the artist, Your colors inspire.
>Said the artist to the poet, Your words are the fire.
>Said the poet to the artist, My tongue is aflame.
>Said the artist to the poet, My brush knows your name.

VI. Left Brain and Right Brain
>Left: Something slithered.   Right: What was it?!
>Left: Something rattled.   Right: Run!

IV. Cygnus

On the Edge of the Lagoon

University of California, Santa Barbara, 1979-1980

W. B. Yeats tallied nine-and-fifty wild swans at Coole.
I count three gulls rooted to the shore of this campus lagoon—
common seabirds, gleaming white and pale gray
still as slack water mirroring a threatening sky.

Damp sand exposes a scroll of scurried prints
a hastily scratched message from the departing flock—
    storm coming!

These three remain, together but apart, heads cocked:
one toward cluttered flotsam, one toward distant thunder,
and one toward plaintive screeching.

Feathers ruffled
by a foretelling breeze
these opportunists choose certainty in the moment.

If scavenging pays, they may stay another day
sheltered by eroding cliff protected from the open sea.
Or they may fly their separate ways.

And I will envision them again and again
recalling that winter on the edge of academic indecision and fear
in my twenty-first year, studying Yeats and Freud

forestalling the inevitable
spring migration.

BASTILLE DAY

So she walked away from herself....
—D. H. Lawrence

In fountain pen ink
she signs the papers
on July fourteenth
declaring her personal freedom.
Not revolt
but revolution
       a turning from
       a turning around.

She had walked away from herself
but now she returns
throws open the door
unlocks the gates
confronts the ruins.

With one long leap

she flies.

WINTER SKY STORIES

Secluded in sulfur springs
they whisper at dusk.
Words hover in rising steam
then float away—
paper lanterns into icy mountain air.
She shivers at each tale
of Black Dog and Blue Devil
twin canine foes that sleep under his skin.
Years ago
they hounded and clawed until his face detached
        slid from his skull
        and fell to the floor
        where it lay
        for months.
She touches his cheek
pressing her wet finger into the dimple where she lives.
"They're not here, now," he reassures her.
Stars glitter in velvet above the opposite ridge.
His eyes twinkle as he smiles.
With left arm around her bare shoulders,
he traces the sky with right forefinger

    Deneb

                Vega

       Altair

the setting Summer Triangle.

The Great Ultimate

He said he could not
        face the future
She said she could not
        face the past
Here they stand
        face to face

Soul to soul.

Note: The yin and yang duality ☯ originates in a consummate oneness known as the Great Ultimate.

MARY PONDERS THE WORD MADE FLESH

for Eddi Porter, thought partner

Young Mary sensed a flutter, felt a wind blow chill.
She wrapped her shawl tighter around her body
and closed her weary eyes against his will.
The angel stood before her, blazing white.
He spoke the humbling message to her doubtful mind
"You will bear a Child on a clear, cold night
and He will be more brilliant than the sun." Kind
Mary kept quiet, frightened by the heavy news.
Though her chest burned and belly yearned
to share the seraph's tidings with some other soul
she "pondered all these things in her heart," we are told.

Would you, too, be so brave and bold
       as not to say
         a word?

LUMINARIAS

...a different kind of light verse....

poems become light
candles, shining, flickering
each essential flame

lunar perfection
unobscured by drifting clouds
white pupil sees black night

imprisoned for verse?
poets write life sentences
they serve time, with love

catalpa trumpets
magenta desert orchids
herald monsoon rain

we are lost humans
celebrating weaponry—
our children, the victims

waging global war
we murder the innocent
mourn only our own

do not extinguish
pillars of light in darkness
poetry must breathe

now more than ever

A Poet's Cairn

*Take up for yourselves twelve stones from the middle of
the river and carry them across. Let this be a sign among
you, so that when your children ask later, "What do
these stones mean to you?" you will answer them.*

Joshua 4:5-7 (paraphrased)

We were the daughters
who called sporadically
      but wrote home often
were independent and resourceful
and hated to ask for money.

We were the older cousins
who said "Let's clean your closet!"
convincing our juniors to remove everything,
and left before putting back a single toy or shoe.

We were the girlfriends in faded photographs
who had accepted boyfriends' just-picked flowers,
tucking the blossoms into our curls
after inspecting for ants and aphids.

We were the mothers
who wielded our sons' baseball bats
against the emptied cardboard moving boxes,
forgot to add flour before baking the brownies
      served them anyway, with spoons
raised our children on Shakespeare and Tolkein
before they were old enough to read for themselves.

We were the visiting aunts
penniless during a Manhattan polar vortex
who slept on the livingroomdiningroomkitchen couches
in married nephews' walk-up apartments.

We were the professors who cared too much,
sometimes not enough,
who wore Santa hats on the last day before winter break
confronting defensive students about plagiarism
comforting others who had suffered a loss.

We descend from strong Jewish grandmothers
who outlived spouses and children
loved us in their own ways
and rejected us when they felt they must.

Now grandparents ourselves
acquainted with grief and joy
we possess wisdom, finally,
after years of partnering and parenting.

We are the poets and artists
responding to global chaos
writing and creating from the inside out.

Inside us are those who have come before—
generations who inhabited lands of burdened promise.
In their footsteps, we contemplate where we have been
question who we are
consider where we are going.

Together
we lift stones from the river
and place them on the other side
to mark our passage.
When our children and grandchildren ask us
we will answer:

We are the ones who survived.

Ordinary Bliss

for Keith

Imperfect February day
almost too warm for skiing.
We drive north on dry two-lane roads
with our two pairs of skis and poles
　　　　　yours antique　　　　mine rented
rattling from the back of the clunker.
I read the newspaper aloud to you.
We nod and shake our heads
at rising unemployment figures
and mortgage defaults.

We sigh at our own good fortune—
no fortune but this—
home and job, two old cars (paid for)
and this Saturday to spend together
celebrating a friend's sixtieth birthday.
The parking area is a muddy mess
but the trailhead looks promising.

Our companions have just buckled on snowshoes
or snapped on skis
so they trudge ahead with the honoree.
It is gray and cloudy.
You watch me struggle through rusty muscle memory,
patiently extend sage advice
　　　　Remember, it's a waltz: ONE two three, PUSH glide glide
before surging ahead in your graceful, practiced rhythm.

I ski alone—
others not too far ahead—
their tracks good company for my clumsy solitude.

Stopping to breathe
and to bandage my blistered heel,
I hear a long ardent moan
emanate from the trees. Listen:
        naked aspens
lean into each other
rubbing bark and limb.
Suddenly, my heart aches,
hoping your tracks stop in the snowy meadow.

As I crest the hill, you turn toward me—
ski poles outstretched—
as if your soul depends on my gliding into view.
I enter your embrace.
You whisper, "Did you hear them, too?"

SHE DID NOT EXPECT

to find a swaying rope cocoon
hot, humid late afternoon
hammock lulls desert girl
mother Caribbean
rocks and hush-a-byes
immutable smoky power
compels white-rimmed surf
cooling ocean breeze
erases memories.
She did not expect rocking chairs
creaking leather, blue-jeans frogs,
or yellow eyelash vipers
masquerading as bromeliads.
Palm fronds chatter island gossip
clouds build gray castles
dusk soon. She did not expect
to hear your voice
carried across the seas.
If you had stepped into this fine sand
instead of the coarse California coast
you would not have survived.
Only blue crabs patrol this black beach
where lacy foam collects around *sargassum* beads
and you call to her.

Igneous Love

Syllable count based on the Fibonacci sequence

Is
a
mountain
covered by
clouds still a mountain?
Veiled Mt. Arenal enshrouds
her fury, a scorned woman whose fiery belly
glows beneath verdant skin. She meditates, planning her
next move. Patient destroyer rests.
Volcano shelters
cacao trees
orchids
snakes
sloths.

Riding a Lazy Horse in Costa Rica

Before I climb the step ladder

to reach his back,

I am introduced to Marlboro

a beautiful chestnut

with neatly trimmed mane and long tail.

Astride, with feet enclosed

in leather stirrups,

I am instructed to blow kisses

loosen the reins

and squeeze my thighs around his middle—

but he is slow to respond.

Marlboro has one speed,

a slow walk,

no matter how much

I kiss and squeeze.

Just like my sixth-grade crush,

this boy knows I'm only pretending—

knows that even as I stroke his neck

I don't really want him to gallop full speed

with me barely hanging on

my body rising and falling

as one with him.

My hesitant touch

meets snorts of lazy approval.

Old Marlboro nips at me—

another biting fly in the cloud forest.

DIVISION OF LABOR

He works
shirtless
in the midmorning sun
preparing the redwood porch swing
with a wire brush and long, smooth strokes
hand sanding
each slat
with the grain.
         She closes her eyes.

He cleans away dust
before upending the swing
to check its hardware.
Matching slot and driver
he secures the back and sides.
         She licks her pen.

He carries the swing to the shade
and pries open the can of stain.
Gloves on, he dips the paintbrush.
         She turns the page.

Looking up from her notebook,
She watches him satisfy
the thirsty wood

while she tightens the screws
of this poem.

V. ORION

SILLY POEM COMPOSED IN TRAFFIC

A string of pearls
A ring of girls
A train of toys
A chain of boys

And so we meet
And love and mate
And so we live
And learn to hate

Until the universe conspires
Teaches lessons
Through the fires
Risks our becoming none the wiser

Flames lick the filth
And sear the wound
Cleanse the will
Anoint the ground

And so we live
And love and mend
Learn to forgive
And learn to bend

A hopeful ray
A joyous day
A flock of geese
To bring us peace

A line of cars
From here to Mars
A life of love
Beneath the stars

HOLDING YOU

Sometimes you loom
redwood tall next to me
face high above
my lifted brow.
Your long limbs
surround me
and I become
not weak, but small
enveloped in tenderness.
I turn my head
press closer
to feel your heart
beat against my cheek.

Other times,
I cradle you
as we lie together
my heart, your pillow
my willow embrace, your comfort
enfolding all of you
into my being
until
incredibly
no longer two
we move
with one breath
a strong
steady
pulse.

LANDLORDS

The tenant Pinyon Jay
alights on the back of our resident eight-point buck
deftly hops
from flank to neck
plucking winter underfur for his nest
      we guess
while the crowned prince
lies unperturbed
certain of his place in nature's hierarchy
lord of the piñon-juniper manor
surveyor of foothill splendor.

The same buck
yesterday
disturbed the doe
reposed in the very hollow
he now occupies.
Alert, she startled
onto all fours
radar ears attuned
to the arroyo.
We watched him watch her,
the points of his antlers
rustling the branches behind
the boulders,
your hand resting lightly
on mine.

LOVE NOTE

for the Sestina sisters

It is impossible
not to stop
mid-breath
when you notice
the three deer
in your yard.

Your rocky yard
presents possible
shelter. The deer
pause, stop
awhile to notice
with alert breath

then settle, breathing,
into the quiet yard.
You notice
a fourth doe, possibly
a fifth, shadowed, stopping
in this place for deer.

These deer
listen, sniff, breathe.
Bucks in velvet stop
in the yard
to rest, possibly,
or to take note.

Sweet love note
spotted fawns, magical deer
make life possible.
Breathe,
measure out yards
of love without stopping.

Why stop
to note
this yard
these deer
whose breath
seems impossible?

Cloistered yard receives those who stop
here in possibility, who notice
the deer, alive in love's breath.

Out to Sea

Moonlit pond
swallows time—
no more day, month, year.
We are here.

Moments sneak into the creek
cascade through narrow canyons—
future rushes past.
We endure.

Histories melt into crackling warmth
a campfire on the riverbank
sparks ascend, become stars.
We touch.

Wounds sting in salt spray
waves wash pain ashore.
An undertow drags the present out to sea.
We heal.

Time dissolves

and all
we have

all we are

is now.

The One That Got Away

I know that loud look on your face—
you heard something
I didn't mean to say.
I want to issue a retraction—
reel it back in. But whatever you heard
is as long gone as the fish
that got away with my rod and reel
when I was ten and deep-sea fishing with my dad—
I was too small
to reach over the hatted heads
of bald fishermen along the starboard rail.
"Probably a bonito or yellow tail," they commiserated.
That fish towed my live anchovy bait,
high tensile line, and lead weight—
pulling the rod from my little fist so fast it burned.
The reel slapped the water in a flash of foam
and disappeared into the deep Pacific
dragged by swimming twisting
downward force
leaving me empty handed
stranded on a fishing boat
the only girl
too timid to shout
too shy to tell a fish story
about the one
that got away.

Under Another Sky

Orion, my protector—
near your diamond belt
a narrow crescent moon
cradles Mars in a stellar nursery.
The Milky Way curves overhead,
a predictable if distant comfort.

A hemisphere away,
my lover sleeps
under another sky.
A disorienting cosmic array
keeps him company
in the Patagonian wilderness
where no city lights outshine the heavens.
Orion, can *you* see him
beneath the Southern Cross?

When he and I shared the
same vast landscape—
tracing our improbable collision course through the galaxy—
we beheld the same constellations.
Even from one hundred miles apart most nights,
we triangulated our being
from a single point in space,
our true North.
But now, Orion,
incalculable isolation
draws me into doubt.
Please hunt for my love
and restore him to me.

PERSPECTIVE

Unlike the infamous
water glass

the moon
is never

    half empty.

Eve, in the *Bosque*

Fat wasp burrows into half-eaten apple.
Desiccated flesh lies exposed beneath leathery red skin.
        Someone has been here before me.

From a wooden bench at the edge of the *bosque*,
I lift my face to the warm autumn sun
and ponder cicada hum.

Far over my shoulder
plein air painter
in lilac sunhat
captures fading sunflowers
supporting a one-cloud sky.

She sees neither wasp nor apple—
painter and poet in parallel
imaginative universes.
Each content
in her own *bosque* world.

Wasp buries thorax
deeper into apple's flesh. And I remember
the sweet sting of your lips.

TASTE THE MORNING

Love is the soul's light, the taste of morning
—Jalal ad-Din Muhammad Rumi

Nothing compares to the taste of this morning
when you awaken to a chorus of coyotes
voicing your soul's longing
from the ravine beyond your open window
and see your lover smiling in half-sleep,
the sheet and the lace-curtain shadows
twisting around his torso
as he turns toward you.

You inhale the barest hint of fall,
a surprising coolness alerts your senses
and you pray
Not yet—
just a few more weeks of pretending it is still summer
when lazy mornings taste of
freshly baked bread, not yet—
just a few more days, hours of heat and pleasure
with nothing to do
but sit and sip iced tea
while Day's yellow dress
skims Earth's brown body.

But with this morning's breath,
you taste the seedy bitterness of coming shorter days
flanked by long, bleak nights
and you wish you could suck the pulpy flesh
of the grape away from thin skin
but it's all or nothing—
pulp, seed, skin together.
No separation this morning.

So you keep your morning ritual
sharing sweet creamy coffee
and warm kisses
tasting the morning
together.

Aging in Tree Pose

Grand, mature cottonwoods
flourish in gold leaf.
Autumn's cobalt dome
protects the yellow canopy
of broad-leafed cottonwoods
in New Mexico,
      my heart's home.
Sharp light, cloudless heaven.
Leafy abundance held aloft by sturdy, gnarled trunk
wrinkled bark, thick limbs, and wide boughs.
Majestic old cottonwoods
      riparian roots
      outstretched arms
embrace the mystery.

To age
is to balance
in tree pose.
Let me be
that ancestral tree
on riverine path
in enchanted autumn—
golden brilliance
reflecting day's last rays

steadfast and serene.

Lotus Moon

Foothill seclusion
above sleeping city
tea-kettle companion
purrs on stove
gas flame
glows

blue lotus
opens
to ascending moon.

ACKNOWLEDGMENTS

Years before we met, a sister New Mexican artist, Meg Leonard, had painted "Silence of the Twilight Dance" as part of a study of light and shadow in the Rio Grande cottonwood *bosque*. When Meg heard me read a draft of "Aging in Tree Pose," she said, "I have the perfect painting for the cover of your next book." Neither of us forgot her prediction. Thank you, Meg. www.megleonard.com

Earlier versions of several poems have appeared elsewhere. A few drafts also debuted on my blog, *In My Own Ink*.

"Aging in Tree Pose" ["Aging"], "The Great Ultimate," and "Ordinary Bliss," in *Poetry from the Other Side,* edited by Chandra Bales, New Mexico State Poetry Society: Albuquerque Chapter, 2013.

"A Footbridge Spans the River of Lost Souls" [as "Patterns on the Bridge"], and some of the "Luminarias," *Small Canyons 8 Anthology*, edited by Jim Applegate, Blue Planet, 2013.

"Eve in the Bosque," in *Poetry in Place: Autumn Writing from the Bosque*, and "Six Short Dialogues," in *Shadow of the Snake*, edited by Jules Nyquist, Poetry Playhouse Publications, 2015.

"Headed North," "Her Chimayo Jacket," "Love Note," "West Coast Summer Moonrise" [as "Lunacy—Large Moon Over Seal Beach"], "Red Pen, Brown Paper," on *In My Own Ink*, pennerink.blogspot.com.

"Lotus Moon" [as "Moonrise above South Crest"] and "Sandia Mountain Lullaby" [as "Mountain Lullaby"] in *Fixed and Free*, edited by Billy Brown, Mercury HeartLink, 2015.

Poetry is also meant to be *heard*. Thank you to the organizers and hosts of community poetry events at which I have read in the last four years:

Adobe Walls/Page One Books, Albuquerque Open Space, Bookworks, Elena Gallegos Open Space, Fixed & Free/The Source, Gallery ABQ, Jules' Poetry Playhouse, The Range, Tractor Brewing, Tortuga Gallery, University of New Mexico Bookstore—all in Albuquerque, NM; Anasazi Fields Winery, Placitas, NM; Artspace Gallery, Tucumcari, NM; a SpAce Gallery, Silver City, NM; UnQuarked Wine Bar, Los Alamos, NM; Rose Keller Library and Community Center, Broadmoor neighborhood, New Orleans, LA; and San Juan College, Farmington, NM.

Finally, I am grateful for all those who read and critiqued the manuscript, in part or whole: Joanne Bodin, Debbie Brody, Kathy Freise, Erin Gallegos, Keith Julian, Meg Leonard, Jules Nyquist, Laura Paine, Susan Paquet, Janet Ruth, Elise Stuart, Chris Turner-Neal, and Stewart Warren. Remaining errors are mine alone.

—Andi Penner, Albuquerque, New Mexico, 2017

ABOUT THE AUTHOR

Andrea (Andi) Penner grew up in southern California, lived for a decade in northern Arizona, and has called New Mexico home since 1994 when she entered the doctoral program in English at the University of New Mexico. In her dissertation, *"The Original In Ourselves": Native American Women Writers and the Construction of Indian Women's Identity*, Andi developed work begun earlier at Northern Arizona University in her Master's thesis, *At Once, Gentle and Powerful: Voices of the Landscape in the Poetry of Luci Tapahonso*. Her essays have appeared in *Studies in American Indian Literature, Teaching English in the Two-Year College*, and *Dead Housekeeping* (an online short-prose publication). Her poems have been selected for *The Rag, Duke City Fix, Conceptions Southwest, Illumina, Epiphany, Northern Arizona Review, Perspectives*, and other publications. *When East Was North* (2012), her first collection of poetry, was published by Mercury Heartlink.

Andi has enjoyed careers in college teaching, education administration, consulting, technical writing, and professoinal communications, and has served as the president of the New Mexico State Poetry Society (2015-2017). She is a founding member of the Crosstown Poets, a supportive writing group dedicated to expanding the reach of poetry in Central New Mexico through readings and workshops.

Made in the USA
Charleston, SC
02 March 2017